Y0-BGH-511

HERDING DOG

A Crabtree Branches Book

B. Keith Davidson

CRABTREE
Publishing Company
www.crabtreebooks.com

School-to-Home Support for Caregivers and Teachers

This high-interest book is designed to motivate striving students with engaging topics while building fluency, vocabulary, and an interest in reading. Here are a few questions and activities to help the reader build upon his or her comprehension skills.

Before Reading:

- *What do I think this book is about?*
- *What do I know about this topic?*
- *What do I want to learn about this topic?*
- *Why am I reading this book?*

During Reading:

- *I wonder why...*
- *I'm curious to know...*
- *How is this like something I already know?*
- *What have I learned so far?*

After Reading:

- *What was the author trying to teach me?*
- *What are some details?*
- *How did the photographs and captions help me understand more?*
- *Read the book again and look for the vocabulary words.*
- *What questions do I still have?*

Extension Activities:

- *What was your favorite part of the book? Write a paragraph on it.*
- *Draw a picture of your favorite thing you learned from the book.*

TABLE OF CONTENTS

What Does a Herding Dog Do?

Herding dogs watch over and guide **livestock** from one place to another. They do this in many ways. Australian cattle dogs nip at the animals' heels. For this reason, these dogs are also called **heelers**. Border collies use what's called a **strong eye**. They stare the animals down.

Australian cattle dog

Border collie

Herding dogs that are kept as pets often try to herd the children of their families.

Australian cattle dog

Why do Dogs Herd Other Animals?

Herding is a trait that comes from dogs' ancestors. Wild dogs such as wolves, African wild dogs, and **dhole** all use similar herding techniques. They move through herds of **prey** and separate the weakest animals from the herd.

wolf

African wild dogs

Dhole

The main job of a herding dog is to guide livestock from one place to another. The animals can then graze in a new area. Guiding the livestock also makes sure the animals avoid fields of valuable crops and busy roads.

Basic Herding Commands

Come- bye: The dog goes to the left of the herd, or clockwise around them.

Away to me: The dog goes to the right of the herd, or counterclockwise around them.

Hold: The dog keeps the livestock where they are.

Find: The dog must go find the livestock.

Herding dogs have exceptional hearing. It allows them to hear commands over the noise of the herd and, during competition, over the noise of the crowd. Their hearing is also important for guarding their livestock from predators, roadways, and other hazards.

 Commands don't always need to be spoken. Handlers use whistles and hand signals to guide the dogs as well.

Breeds

Border Collies

There are many different types of sheepdog, but the border collie is one of the most well-known. When these dogs enter competitions, they often win.

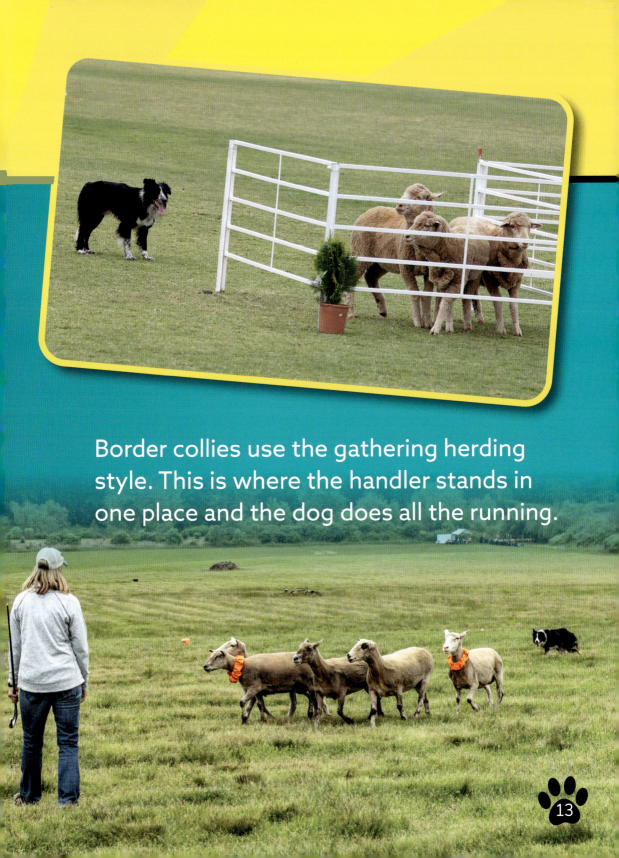

Border collies use the gathering herding style. This is where the handler stands in one place and the dog does all the running.

Australian Cattle Dogs

Blue heelers, red heelers, the Queensland heeler, and the Texas heeler are all Australian cattle dogs. These dogs are related to Australia's **dingoes**.

Dingo

Blue heeler

Red Australian shepherd

Queensland heeler

Australian Shepherds

Australian Shepherds were first bred in the 1800s in the United States—not Australia.

Kelpies and Koolies

The Australian kelpie and Australian koolie are breeds known for walking on the backs of sheep to keep them in line. They also use the heeler biting technique as well as the staring technique used by **headers**, like border collies. That's why kelpies' and koolies' style of herding is called head, heel, and back.

Australian kelpie

Australian koolie

FACT Why did the kelpie walk on the backs of its flock? To get to the other side. It's not a great joke, but it's true. Sometimes in a tightly packed pen, it's the easiest way to travel.

Picking the Perfect Puppy

A puppy that *wants* to herd things should be chosen to become a herder. Herding should be a natural **instinct** in the dog.

Herding dogs are sometimes out with the livestock on their own, without handlers. That makes it extra important that the dogs enjoy doing this type of work.

 **FACT** How do you know if a dog herds? It'll likely herd you! This is just one of the ways that a dog can show you that it is ready to herd.

Training

A herding puppy's training starts with it being introduced to a herd on a long leash. The dog is rewarded if it's calm around the herd.

A puppy may be **intimidated** by cows, so many trainers start with chickens to let the dog get comfortable.

After being introduced, the handler walks the dog through other commands on a short leash. The commands show the dog how it is allowed to **interact** with the animals.

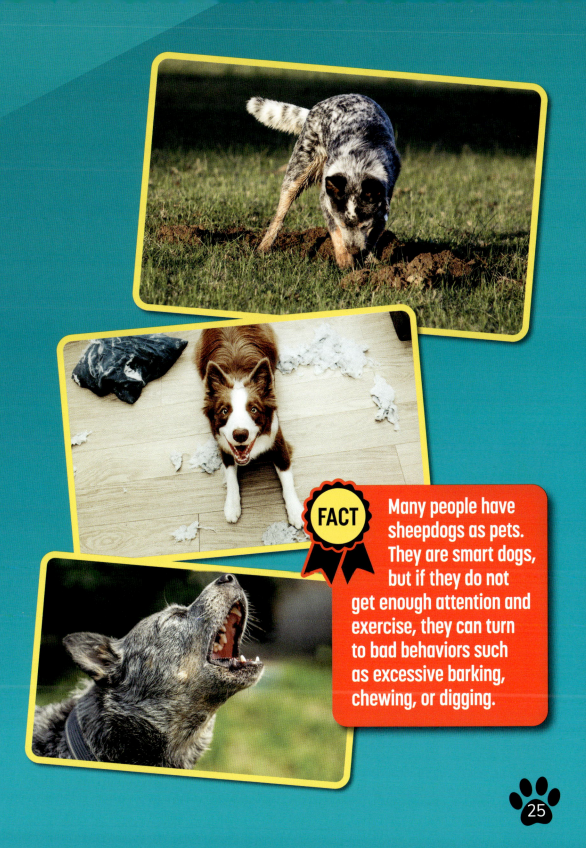

FACT Many people have sheepdogs as pets. They are smart dogs, but if they do not get enough attention and exercise, they can turn to bad behaviors such as excessive barking, chewing, or digging.

The Herding Dog World Champions!

Yes, herding is a competitive sport, and has been since the 1800s. There are local, national, and even the World Sheepdog Trials, held by the International Sheep Dog Society (ISDS). These competitions are serious business, and the winners can earn their owners a lot of money.

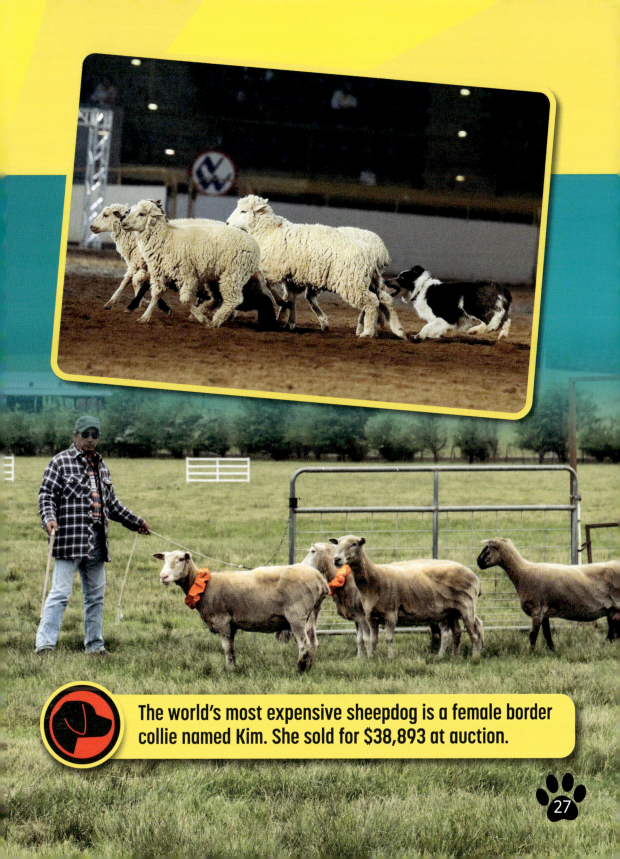

The world's most expensive sheepdog is a female border collie named Kim. She sold for $38,893 at auction.

The competing dogs must run with their flock through an obstacle course. They show the judges different skills, such as leading sheep in and out of a pen, separating a marked sheep from the flock, and getting the sheep to stay in one spot. The whole time, they're being timed and judged on style.

At the 2020 ISDS World Championships, there were 238 competitors from 29 different countries.

Glossary

dhole (DOLE): a type of wild dog that lives in Asia

dingoes (ding-GOEZ): wild dogs of Australia

header (hed-UR): a dog that stares down the sheep

heelers (heel-URZ): dogs that nip at the heels of livestock to keep them in check

instinct (IN-stingkt): behavior that is natural rather than learned

interact (in-tur-AKT): describes action between people, groups, or animals

intimidated (in-TIM-uh-dated): frightened or scared by something

livestock (LIVE-stok): animals who are born and raised on farms

prey (PRAY): animals that are hunted and eaten by other animals

strong eye (STRONG I): a technique where a herding dog gets in front of the livestock and stares at them to keep them in line

Index

Websites to Visit

https://easyscienceforkids.com/all-about-sheep-dogs/

https://kids.kiddle.co/Sheep_dog

https://kids.britannica.com/kids/article/sheepdog/477009

About the Author

B. Keith Davidson

B. Keith Davidson grew up around dogs and has always been fascinated by the bonds that humans and these very special creatures share. Beagles are his favorite dogs, even if they are stubborn and frustrating. He has a Master's degree in Canadian History from Carleton University.

CRABTREE
Publishing Company

Written by: B. Keith Davidson
Designed by: Jennifer Dydyk
Edited by: Kelli Hicks
Proofreader: Janine Deschenes

Photographs: Cover illustration of Dog(also on title page) © Nevada3, photo of dog with sheep © Ann Tyurina, Page 4 © Elton Abreu, Page 5 top photo © Shaun Barr, bottom photo © Kim Reinick, Page 6 © Sergey Uryadnikov, Page 7 top photo © Rudi Hulshof, bottom photo © Independent birds, Page 8 © Ann Tyurina, Page 9 top photo © Joe Dunckley, bottom photo © S1001, Page 10 © The Old Major, Page 11 top photo © alens, bottom photo © Shaun Barr, Page 12 © Lisjatina, Page 13 top photo © clearviewstock, bottom photo © Cynthia Liang, Page 14 © Wright Out There, Blue Heeler and Queensland Heeler photos © TanyaCPhotography, Australian Shepherd © Vesna Kriznar, Page 16 © Vineyard Perspective, Page 17 kelpie © bazilpp, koolie © TanyaCPhotography, Page 18 © Alexandra Kruspe, Page 19 top photo © Martin Charles Hatch, bottom photo © Dora Zett, Page 20 top photo © Zuzule, bottom photo © chloe edwards, Page 21 top photo © Dora Zett, bottom photo © dm-visign, Page 22 © thka, Page 23 chickens © Janon Stock, puppy © etreeg, Page 24 © Dora Zett, Page 25 top photo © Madelein Wolfaardt, middle photo © smrm1977, bottom photo © ms.yenes, Page 26 © top photo © Dana Ward, Page 27 top photo © photo-denver, photo across Page 26 and Page 27 and Page 28 and Page 29 top photo © Cynthia Liang, Page 29 bottom photo © ClimbWhenReady. All images from Shutterstock.com

Library and Archives Canada Cataloguing in Publication

CIP available at Library and Archives Canada

Library of Congress Cataloging-in-Publication Data

CIP available at Library of Congress

Crabtree Publishing Company

www.crabtreebooks.com   1-800-387-7650

Copyright © 2022 **CRABTREE PUBLISHING COMPANY**   Printed in the U.S.A./CG20210915/012022

Published in the United States
Crabtree Publishing
347 Fifth Avenue, Suite 1402-145
New York, NY, 10016

Published in Canada
Crabtree Publishing
616 Welland Ave.
St. Catharines, Ontario L2M 5V6